SOUL BE FREE

VOICES FROM THE VALLEY OF DRY BONES

SOUL BE FREE

VOICES FROM THE VALLEY OF DRY BONES

ALFONSO WYATT & OUIDA C. WYATT

Copyright © 2022 by Strategic Destiny, LLC.

All rights reserved. Except permitted under the U.S. Copyright Act of 1976, no part of this publication may be used, reproduced, distributed or transmitted by in any form or by any means, graphic, electronic or mechanical or stored in a database or retrieval system, without the prior written permission to the publisher except in the case of brief quotations embodied in critical articles and reviews.

Unless otherwise indicated, Scriptures are taken from the Holy Bible, New International Version®, NIV® Copyright © 1973, 1978, 1984, 2011 by Biblica, Inc.™ Used by permission. All rights reserved worldwide.

Strategic Destiny's name and logo are trademarks of Strategic Destiny, LLC.

ISBN: 978-0-9982566-1-0 (paperback)

Library of Congress Cataloging-in-Publication Data
Library of Congress Control Number: 2022917883

Published by Strategic Destiny, LLC.
New York, NY

Printed in the United States of America

This book is dedicated to sisters and brothers who may find themselves trapped in The Valley of Dry Bones, or fighting to leave.
May your voices be heard; may your efforts be rewarded.

TABLE OF CONTENTS

FOREWORD...IX

PSALM 13..1

    THORN...3
    clear vision..5
    LAMENTATION..6
    SCARRED..7
    invitation..9
    Riff..11

PSALM 37..13

    DISCONNECTED...15
    just believe..16
    STORM CLOUDS...18
    oh my child..20
    rainbow truth...22
    Riff..23

PSALM 29..25

    soliloquy..27
    SEEK PEACE..28
    cry...29

ANGELS LOST AND FOUND ... 31
BEATITUDE ATTITUDE ... 32
Riff ... 34

PSALM 23 ... 35

final voyage ... 37
DRY BONES CHRONICLES ... 38
true confession ... 39
DRY SOUL ... 41
knock knock ... 43
Riff ... 44

SOUL FUEL ... 45
VALLEY OF DRY BONES QUESTIONS FOR REFLECTION/INSIGHT ... 49
EZEKIEL 37 ... 53
BENEDICTION ... 55
NOTES ... 56
BOOKS BY THE AUTHORS ... 59

*Poems in upper case created by OCW
*Poems in lowercase created by AW

FOREWORD

DR. JAMES A. FORBES JR.

Senior Minister Emeritus
Riverside Church

This is unusual
that dry bones
in the Valley
would be able to voice
their sense of
frustration and despair
Nevertheless
God hears their complaint
The bones are saying
we are dry
our hope is lost
we are clean cut off
No matter our situation
God is able to hear
and understand
our plight
The God who helps
is able to give
a promise of
remediation and repair
The God who hears
is also
the God
of
hope

PSALM 13

*How long, Lord?
Will you forget me
forever?
How long
will you hide
your face from me?
How long
must I wrestle
with my thoughts
and
day after day
have sorrow in my heart?
How long
will my enemy
triumph over me?
Look on me and answer,
Lord my God.
Give light to my eyes,
or
I will sleep in death,
and
my enemy will say,
"I have overcome him,"
and my foes will rejoice
when I fall.
But
I trust in your unfailing love;
my heart rejoices in your salvation.
I will sing the Lord's praise,
for he has been good to me.*

THORN

HOW WILL YOU DESCRIBE
THE THORN IN YOUR SIDE
        AS A MOUNTAIN TO CLIMB
        OR
        A ROCK WALL
        IN FRONT OF YOU
        THE THING THAT
        KEEPS YOU UP AT NIGHT
        AND AT DAYBREAK
        SEEMS TO INTENSIFY
        ELECTRIC SHOCKS
        TO EVERY JOINT
        WHEN YOU ARE STILL
        LEGS AND ARMS
        HAVE A MIND
        OF THEIR OWN
                        HOW WILL YOU DESCRIBE
                        THE THORN IN YOUR SIDE
        WANT TO RUN
        BUT
        CAN'T WALK
        WANT TO SHOUT
        BUT
        CAN'T TALK
        CRITICAL OR CHRONIC TREATMENT
        BY PILL OR TONIC
        NOW FEELING PRESSURE
        ACROSS YOUR BROW
        OUT OF BALANCE

JUST ONE MORE CHALLENGE
IN THE DISTANCE
HEAR A STILL SMALL VOICE
MY GRACE IS SUFFICIENT
I AM OMNISCIENT
HOLD
ON

clear vision

the me i see
hides in me
the me i see
prone to flee
the me i see
afraid to be

                              the me i see
                       fought hard for me
                              the me i see
                           challenges me
                              the me i see
                         wants the best
                                    for me

the me i see
grows strong in me
the me i see
no longer scares me
the me i see
has a vision for me

LAMENTATION

CONSTERNATION ISOLATION
DREAD
WHO ARE THESE VOICES
RUNNING AROUND
IN MY HEAD
POWER BEING BLOCKED
THE MUNDANE TABLE IS SPREAD
DISTRACTING MY FOCUS
FROM LOOKING UP
WHEN WILL I BREAK AWAY
FROM THIS BITTER CUP
I BELIEVE
THE PROPHECY
SPOKEN
WILL BE MINE
THE WORD
FOR MY LIFE
AN APPOINTED
TIME

SCARRED

CUT DEEP
BUT SPARED TO SEE
ANOTHER DAY
TO REVEAL
JUST HOW I CAME
TO REALLY DEAL
WITH MY PAIN
COUNTING THE TIMES
I HAVE BEEN DOWN
BUT NOT OUT
DO
I
REJECT
      REFLECT
           RESPECT
BEING SCARRED
SEEING DAILY
THE MARKS
THE VISIBLE PATTERNS
I COUNT OFF
HERE
HERE
AND
HERE
SCARRED
NOT BARRED
FROM DIFFICULTY
YOU SEE
HE WAS WOUNDED

FOR OUR TRANSGRESSIONS
NOT HIS OWN
WHEN I SEE
HIS NAILED SCARRED HAND
I KNOW
I
LIVE
TO
PROCLAIM
HIS
RIGHTEOUS
NAME

invitation

come to the edge

get closer to your fears
mired in anxiety
wrapped in trauma
the voice in your head
warns you away
    continuing
years and years
      of
practiced avoidance
you move but manage
to stay in place

                come to the edge

                  the route
            already worked out
as you try to find your way out
      there is a path my friend
              it is found
           not by thinking
                but
           by searching
    the edge is not the end
        as the whisperer
          convinced you
       it is the beginning
         as your spirit
         will show you

if only you
would

                                                come to the edge

        new mind

            new thought

                new awakening

new spirit

      new revelation

           new you

There is a high price being paid by people who take what is new and force it to become a servant of what is old. New has to fight for space while old takes up space. New offers visions of what can be while old can only replay what was. New pulls the best out of us while old settles for what it can get.

PSALM 37:1-8

Do not fret

*because of those who are evil
or be envious*

of those who do wrong;

for like the grass

*they will soon wither,
like green plants*

they will soon die away.

*Trust in the Lord and do good;
dwell in the land*

and

*enjoy safe pasture.
Take delight in the Lord,
and*

he will give you

the desires of your heart.

*Commit your way to the Lord;
trust in him and he will do this:
He will make your righteous reward*

*shine like the dawn,
your vindication like the noonday sun.*

*Be still before the Lord
and wait patiently for him;
do not fret*

when people succeed

*in their ways,
when they carry out*

their wicked schemes.

Refrain from anger

and

*turn from wrath;
do not fret—it leads*

only to evil.

DISCONNECTED

NO SATISFACTION
FOR AN UNYIELDED SOUL
GIFTED WANDERER
WITH
NO REAL DIRECTION
DOING
FOR SELF
TO SELF
BUT WILL NOT GIFT
TO ANYONE
ELSE
CIRCLING CIRCLING
JUST
CIRCLING
NOT SERVING
DISAPPEARING
INTO
SELF ABYSS
YOU MISS
THERE ARE FOLK
WHO COULD GAIN
FROM YOUR GIVING
BUT
DO THINGS
REALLY MATTER
IF
IT
ONLY
SERVES
YOU

just believe

this is the darkest
of days
my fears realized
captured by your words
we must part
over and over
through long
nights
my heart seeks
what went wrong
how could this love
be so misunderstood
our bond
stood strong
against pretense
remember how
we   laughed
we   cried
we   grew
apart
fate
intertwined two lives
sharing
baring
holding
each other
now
can't let go
for the bond

            still strong
             believe
              in me
             believe
             in self
    just   believe

STORM CLOUDS

ROLL ON THE RIVER CAREGIVER

THE EVER-RISING TIDE
UPON YOU
ROLL ON THE RIVER CAREGIVER

EACH DAY BRINGS ANOTHER
FRAUGHT WITH THE EBB AND FLOW
OF NEEDS
STORM CLOUDS OVERHEAD
DOING DAILY
WHAT IT TAKES
TO STAY AFLOAT
THE MISSION
TO STAND
AND
WITHSTAND
FOR THOSE
WHO CAN NO LONGER
DO FOR THEMSELVES

ROLL ON THE RIVER CAREGIVER
THERE IS PROVISION
IN THE PRESSING
WHILE ADDRESSING
THE CALL
TO POUR
OUT
WHAT WAS POURED

INTO YOU
FOR THE ALMIGHTY
NAVIGATOR
WILL SEE
YOU
THROUGH

oh my child

what of my child's dreams
                    borne aloft
                by the innocence
                  of wanting
              cotton candy clouds
                gum drop stars
                                          playing forever

what of my child's dreams
                    to be rich
                    no more
                hungry nights
                      or
                pointless days
                                        escaping forever

what of my child's dreams
                the realization
                      life
                      and
                  nightmares
                      are
                      the
                    same
                                        damned forever

what of my child's dreams
            reflections of dream death
                first borne aloft
                      by

　　　　the
　　　innocence
　　　　 of
　　　 wanting
　　　　　　　　　　　　　　　　gone forever

rainbow truth

look outside
grey clouds
disperse
where there once was
doom and gloom
god's colorful light
arc the sky

life is that way
rain then sun
sun then rain

there can never
be a
rainbow
if the sun refused
to shine
through
the mist of life
hide this truth
deep
    in your soul

JESUS CAME
TO SEEK AND SAVE
THE ADVERSARY
TO STEAL AND DESTROY
SEEK YE FIRST
FLEE THE CURSE
STRUCK DOWN
BUT NOT
DESTROYED

The relationship to self, to others, and to God is what gives life its value. When we examine what our experiences teach us, we no longer label them good or bad. These lessons reveal the spiritual stamina gained from our physical trials. Whether sunshine, rain, heartache, or pain, we can rise because of the soul seeded deep inside.

PSALM 29:1-9

Ascribe to the LORD,

*you heavenly beings,
ascribe to the LORD*

*glory and strength.
Ascribe to the LORD*

*the glory due his name;
worship the LORD in the splendor*

of his holiness.

The voice of the LORD

*is over the waters;
the God of glory thunders,
the LORD thunders over the mighty waters.
The voice of the LORD*

*is powerful;
the voice of the LORD*

*is majestic.
The voice of the LORD*

*breaks the cedars;
the LORD breaks in pieces*

*the cedars of Lebanon.
He makes Lebanon leap like a calf,
Sirion like a young wild ox.
The voice of the LORD*

*strikes
with flashes of lightning.
The voice of the LORD*

*shakes the desert;
the LORD shakes*

*the Desert of Kadesh.
The voice of the LORD*

*twists the oaks
and strips the forests bare.
And in his temple*

all cry, "Glory!"

soliloquy

life at times
senseless to me
why must I live
quasi-free
what natural law
did i violate
now tied to this
discouraging fate
running in shadows
spurning the light
asking who really knows
what is right
years of resisting
deep self-hate
serves to further
deflate
what
dignity
left inside
while holding fast
to
fleeting pride
my pain is there
for all to see
blackness
me
or
this
country

SEEK PEACE

PEACE IS PROFOUND
BUT
WON'T STICK AROUND
MUST BE PURSUED
ESCAPE FROM BAD MOODS
ANTICIPATE
NOT
DISSIPATE
PLUNGED TO DEEP PEACE
AT
THE CENTER
OF A
STORM
NOT OUT OF YOUR GRASP
SEEK PEACE
HOPE
AT
LAST

cry

tears
soul libation
for ancestors
snatched
in
the
night

tears
soul libation
for hapless people
lost
in
babylon

tears
soul libation
mourning how
good it used to be
fully knowing
it
never
was
tears
soul libation
this body
quakes as

i
cry
for
me

ANGELS LOST AND FOUND

ANGELS LOST AND FOUND
GLIMPSES OF LIGHT REFLECTING
OFF THE GROUND
COME UP HIGH
TO THE
ENERGY SOURCE
WITHOUT JUDGMENT
FLEE REMORSE
ANGELS LOST AND FOUND
SET YOUR GAZE
ON HIGHER GROUND
MOVE OUT FROM ORDINARY
TIME AND SPACE
TO THE EXTRAORDINARY
BY
TRANSFORMING GRACE
ANGELS LOST AND FOUND
NOW LOOKING UP
NOT WEIGHED DOWN
MAKING CONNECTIONS
FOR OTHERS MUST SEE
THEY HAVE THIS TREASURE
THAT WILL
SET
YOU
FREE

BEATITUDE ATTITUDE

BLESSED YOU ARE

BLESSED WHEN YOU
HEAR THE PROPHETIC
WORD
SPOKEN
TO
YOU

                      BLESSED YOU ARE

                      BLESSED WHEN YOU
                RECEIVE EVERY PROMISE
                        GIFTS GIVEN
                              TO
                            YOU

                                            BLESSED YOU ARE

                                      BLESSED WHEN YOU
                                      BELIEVE THE GOD
                                              OF LOVE
                                    WORKS ALL THINGS
                                          TOGETHER
                                                FOR
                                                YOU

BLESSED YOU ARE

BLESSED WHEN YOU
KNOW
JESUS SACRIFICE
PREPARES
A
PLACE
FOR
YOU

life
flows
along
destiny's
riverbed
each ripple
time
no
more

All accomplishments in life, good, bad, or indifferent can happen only in the course of time. It has been said that time is money; I would like to amend this statement and say that time is valuable. Are you investing your time properly? Do you see a return on your time investment? Is your time spent complaining, daydreaming, finding enemies—or are you taking time to find your true self? That, beloved, is time well spent.

PSALM 23

The Lord is my shepherd, I lack nothing.
He makes me lie down in green pastures,
he leads me beside quiet waters,
he refreshes my soul.

He guides me along the right paths
for his name's sake.
Even though I walk
through the darkest valley,
I will fear no evil,
for you are with me;
your rod and your staff,
they comfort me.

You prepare a table before me
in the presence of my enemies.
You anoint my head with oil;
my cup overflows.

Surely your goodness and love
will follow me all the days of my life,
and I will dwell
in the house of the LORD
forever.

final voyage

hold fast the stern
in life's sea
sail on to
meet your destiny
fated ship is tossed about
towering waves overwhelm
with doubt
no compass to
chart a saving course
in raging storm
at full force
prayers to god
given in fear
roaring wind
is all you hear
thoughts of when
you were young
idyllic times
filled with fun
honored vows
goals yet to be made
all begin to slowly fade
living colors
turn mournful grey
there are
no more noble
words
to
say

DRY BONES CHRONICLES

FEELING DECIMATED
GOT TO
FOCUS
ON WHAT CAN BE
IT'S BEEN
SUFFOCATED
BUT CAN IT BE
REVIVED
TRACE STEPS BACK
TO WHEN
THE GOOD GROUND
STARTED SHOWING CRACKS
WHEN WILL THE RAINS COME
MOOD SWINGS
BUT
CAN'T BRING MYSELF
TO THE POINT
OF
GIVING UP
I SILENCE THE
VOICES
BY
SPEAKING
LIFE

true confession

dear lord

i thank you

        for assurance
        yet i still give in to my doubts

                lord forgive me

i thank you

        for love
        yet i still cannot love all of me

                lord forgive me

i thank you

        for wisdom
        yet i still cling to ignorance

                lord forgive me

i thank you

        for direction
        yet i still find myself lost

                lord forgive me

i thank you

        for hope
        yet i still live in fear

                lord forgive me

the lord's response
there is an inner war raging
flesh against spirit
each time you cry
each time you pray
i help you mediate

assurance/doubt
love/self-hate
wisdom/ignorance
direction/lost
hope/fear
so my child
don't beg for forgiveness
pray for power
to
overcome

DRY SOUL

MEND IT DON'T END IT
                              THERE IS SOMETHING
                              JUST AROUND THE BEND
                              RIGHT NOW
                              NO WAY OUT
                              HITTING WALL AFTER WALL
                              ALL PATHS BLOCKED
                              STRETCHED SO THIN
                              NO LIGHT GETTING IN
                              MIGHT AS WELL DEPART
                              CANNOT CONCEIVE
                              A RESTART
                                                          MEND IT DON'T END IT
                              TRULY AN EVEREST TO CLIMB
                              REACHING UP
                              IS THERE
                              A HAND TO GRAB
                              SHOUTING LOUD
                              WHILE
                              SINKING
                              DROWNING
                              SEE PAST
                              THE FALSE FAÇADE
                              NEED RESCUE
                              RESTORING HYDRATION
                              TO THIS DRY SOUL
MEND IT DON'T END IT

OVER THE HORIZON
NEW
LIFE
RISING

knock knock

oh no
trouble at
my door
ominous knock
hard to ignore
how it makes me
cringe each night
filled with foreboding
gripped by fright
what new pain will you
bring today
causing my resolve
to further fray
is it your wish
to control my mind
pushing me over
sanity's line
that separates those
who can and do
from those who have
succumbed to you
the next time
you knock
at this door
know i ain't
opening it
anymore

TENSION
UNIDENTIFIED
RAW EMOTION
MENTALLY EXHAUSTED
OCEAN DEEP
INTENTION
LOVE

Every person with a pulse will experience the changing seasons. The vicissitudes of life find us making our way across chasms great and small. We lay bare the narrative so it does not overtake us. Release, feel, acknowledge—then continue for truly it is life that awaits so journey on.

SOUL FUEL

1. *Forgetting those things which are behind and straining for what is up ahead, I press toward the mark of the high calling in Christ Jesus…*   *(Philippians 3:13-14)*

2. *So do not fear, for I am with you, do not be dismayed, for I am your God. I will strengthen you and help you; I will uphold you with my righteous right hand. (Isaiah 41:10)*

3. *We are hard pressed on every side, but not crushed; perplexed, but not in despair; persecuted but not abandoned; struck down, but not destroyed. (2 Cor 4: 8-9)*

4. *"Come to me, all you who are weary and burdened, and I will give you rest. Take my yoke upon you and learn from me, for I am gentle and humble in heart, and you will find rest for your souls." (Matthew 11:28-29)*

5. *Who shall separate us from the love of Christ? Shall trouble, or hardship, persecution or famine or nakedness or danger or sword… No in all things we are more than conquerors through Him who loves us. (Romans 8:35)*

6. *As it is written: No, in all these things we are more than conquerors through him who loved us. For I am convinced that neither death nor life, neither angels nor demons, neither the present nor the future, nor any powers, neither height nor depth, nor anything else in all creation, will be able to separate us from the love of God that is in Christ Jesus our Lord. (Romans 8: 37-39)*

7. *"Do you want to be made well?" (John 5: 6)*

8. *"And why do you worry about clothes? See how the flowers of the field grow. They do not labor or spin. Yet I tell you that not even Solomon in all his splendor was dressed like one of these. If that is how God clothes the grass of the field, which is here today and tomorrow is thrown into the fire, will he not much more clothe you…?"*   *(Matthew 6:28-30)*

9. ...greater is he that is in you, than he that is in the world. (1 John 4:4a)

10. "Blessed are they that mourn for they shall be comforted." (Matthew 5:4)

VALLEY OF DRY BONES QUESTIONS FOR REFLECTION/INSIGHT

1. Was there a voice (poem) In The Valley of Dry Bones that spoke to you? If so, what did you hear?

   _____

   _____

   _____

2. Do you have any thoughts as to why some people stay in The Valley of Dry Bones longer than they should?

   _____

   _____

   _____

3. Can you recall a time when you were in The Valley of Dry Bones? If so, what pulled you in; how did you get out?

   _____

   _____

   _____

4. What role, if any, does fear, doubt, or pride play in muting Voices in The Valley of Dry Bones?

   _____

   _____

   _____

5. What are your thoughts about generations of family members trapped in The Valley of Dry Bones?

_____

_____

_____

6. Do you have a Valley of Dry Bones "life lesson" that you learned while trapped and still live by; if so, what was your life lesson?

_____

_____

_____

7. If you have a loved one, or a friend in The Valley of Dry Bones, which one of the voices do you think he or she would benefit hearing?

_____

_____

_____

The hand of the LORD was upon me, and he brought me out by the Spirit of the LORD and set me in the middle of a valley; it was full of bones. He led me back and forth among them, and I saw a great many bones on the floor of the valley, bones that were very dry. He asked me, "Son of man, can these bones live?" I said, "O Sovereign LORD, you alone know." Then he said to me, "Prophesy to these bones and say to them, 'Dry bones, hear the word of the LORD! This is what the Sovereign LORD says to these bones: I will make breath enter you, and you will come to life.'"

Ezekiel 37: 1-5

BOOKS BY THE AUTHORS

Soul Be Free Prose Poems Prayers

Soul Be Free II

Soul Be Free III: Different Hues of The Blues

Mentoring From The Inside Out: Healing Boys Transforming Men

Leadership By Numbers: For God's People Who Count

Before You Jump The Broom Clean Up Your Room

Madd Truth: Lasting Lessons for Students of Life

Beware The Mind Hustler: Identifying Self Destructive Thoughts And Distractions

(Books can be purchased online via Amazon/Barnes & Noble)

• • • • • • • •

New Wine In New Wineskins: Post COVID-19 Church Organizational Development & Leadership Manual

(Email order to alfonsowyatt09@gmail.com)

www.ingramcontent.com/pod-product-compliance
Lightning Source LLC
Chambersburg PA
CBHW070439010526
44118CB00014B/2117